more than the score...

JOHN CAGE

In a Landscape

for piano solo

Presented by Adam Tendler

Contents

Adam Tendler talks about Cage's *In a Landscape*	2
In a Landscape	5
About the composer	14
About the music	14

EDITION PETERS
PUBLISHED BY FABER MUSIC
Leipzig · London · New York

This edition © 2017 by Peters Edition Ltd, London

Adam Tendler
talks about
John Cage's *In a Landscape*

This piece has a rigid rhythmic structure. It's 15x15: that's 15 bars of music separated into five bars, seven bars, three bars. Sometimes we might hear that, as in the opening – where we really do have a clear phrase. Later in the piece, the music tends to blend between those structural barriers.

There are many different examples of phrasing in *In a Landscape*. It begins with short phrases, or short phrase markings. I think of them as slurs in the very beginning in the left hand. We can think of this as a series of short slurs, or we can think of them as a longer line, a longer melody, that leads to that final A.

A lot of the textures tend to overlap in this piece and their roles overlap, too. The score will indicate that a certain note should be more of a melody note, really on top of an accompaniment figure. This happens right at the very beginning with the two repeated B flats. Somehow, these have to be two different notes: one is more prevalent, one is our accompaniment figure.

There are points where these overlapping figures create a real task for the pianist to delineate between the phrases, the accompaniment phrase and the melody phrase. We have a melody in the right hand and an accompanying phrase in the left hand, and the right hand begins to creep into the left-hand area. We have to create a difference within a very soft dynamic range.

Rubato and counting

In a piece that is so rigidly structured, rhythmically, but also pleasing and outwardly beautiful, there is a fine line between not sprinkling too much rubato into it, but making it an expressive piece of music – which, to me, it really is.

For a piece that, on first hearing or even on first playing, may seem very repetitive, the more time we spend with *In a Landscape*, the more we can discover its variety. Different melodic sections may reappear, but they may appear at a different part of a bar, and where a section may have started on beat 1 and has a very strong first beat, later it might come in on beat 3. A pianist who spends time with this piece will discover this, and these variations will help to define the different sections and where the dynamics may differ. It helps to count constantly through this piece so as to discover these moments. The first treble melody we hear happens on a strong first beat: it's hard to miss this beautiful moment.

The metronome marking of 80 is an invitation to keep the piece moving. Reigning in the rubato and keeping it in the context of a strong metronomic beat keeps the music going and prevents us from getting lost in this landscape.

Dynamics

This piece is mostly a soft piece: the loudest it ever gets is *mezzoforte*, according to the score. We begin with everything marked *pianissimo* and the pianist has to make a choice as to whether or not one hand is a melody and the other is an accompaniment.

Later in the piece, Cage writes out different dynamic shadings; for instance, the right hand here is *piano* and the left hand is *pianissimo*. In a piece that's always within the soft dynamic, that difference is rather significant and we need to take note of it.

In bars 108–110, we have tenuto left-hand notes that conflict with the right-hand phrases. Then, at bar 111, we hit our loudest

> *The more time we spend with* In a Landscape, *the more we can discover its variety*

dynamic. It's good to note that this *mezzoforte* is your peak, dynamically speaking, of the piece.

Grace notes

There are a couple of very expressive, beautiful, but pianistically awkward grace notes in this piece, and different people may approach them different ways. I tend to view them rather classically. I think in Classical music, or Baroque music, an ornament or grace note is subordinate. What's more important is the larger melodic line, and so with *In a Landscape* I always try to think of what is the big note, what is the note that this grace note is decorating. In bar 38, it's tempting to want to bring the grace notes out – and we could, but I think what's more important is that, when this phrase repeats just a few bars later, Cage leaves the grace notes out. I want us to hear that there's a relationship between these, not one is totally different from the other when it repeats. So when I do it first with the grace note, I try to keep the integrity of the larger more melodic fragment. But this may change over time: that's the beauty of a work with the depth of *In a Landscape*: every time you come back to it, you may have totally different thoughts on it.

Later on, in bar 41, I would resist the temptation to bring out this grace note. I'm more concerned with the continuation of the melody than with spiking the grace note. It's not about that F, it's really about the D.

John Cage. Photographer unknown. Courtesy of the John Cage Trust

Distribution of parts

Different pianists will approach this piece physically in different ways that suit their hands, whether they have big hands or small hands. I tend to distribute parts between the hands as I feel serves the phrase, but also how it serves my comfort. There's one triplet in this piece – in bar 105 – and it ushers in a melody, but requires a little bit of a quick turnaround. It's at the end of the octave phrase so I quickly move my left hand to that triplet. I let my left hand take the first three notes and I have my right hand finish its phrase. And, in a matter of a second, my left hand goes from having a melodic role to an accompaniment role and, again, the hands are very close together. There has to be this real management of the parts. They're right on top of each other.

Tenuto

Tenuto markings are sprinkled throughout this piece. I think these give the pianist an indication of where the weight should go, whether or not the notes with tenuto marks even form part of a melody. I don't know if that translates to a sense of loudness, because we really do have to keep things within a quiet dynamic.

In bar 136, we have dark, brooding left-hand chords with tenuto markings – and they're rather dissonant in the context of the piece. We have three tenuto marks. Again, I don't think that means they have to be loud because that's going to distract the whole arc of the piece – and it's only *mezzopiano* – but the pianist should keep in mind that there are tenutos here and that it's OK to approach them with weight.

Even in passages with uniform dynamics, like the opening of the piece, the tenuto can help guide us physically and it can help guide our ear in terms of what we should focus on. So, for the left-hand tenuto on the A at the very opening of the piece, it's crucial for us to know that this has a different role from phrasing.

When we're faced with rising scale patterns, we can often succumb to the temptation to speed up but also to raise our dynamic. Often, in this piece, these rising scale patterns are phrased, so we should actually, in my view, taper off. In the passage beginning at bar 141, you have different phrases beginning at different times and we have to keep the dynamic floating away, and also keep the tempo in check.

Harmonic language

We might think of this piece as an exploration of, say, a B flat major seven chord, but Cage also introduces the B natural which keeps recurring in the treble – and we also get Gs throughout. So this piece functions within a limited gamut of notes, but Cage finds incredibly inventive ways to keep us interested and to keep the piece full of variety. He also saves one pitch – the E – for the chiming passage which first appears at bar 91, and it does sound rather new to our ear. It's a really special moment in the piece, one that our ear remembers.

The ending

From bar 216, Cage repeats the ascending scale phrase six times. In the first three there's no decrescendo, but of course it's rather soft. In the last three repeats he wants us to taper our dynamic. The way I think of approaching the harmonics in the final bar is that I want the silently depressed chord to actually match the dynamics of my decrescendo. It actually gives me a goal, dynamically speaking, within that section – not just to get soft, indefinitely soft and trying to get as soft as possible: I want it to actually match what's going to come later. It's also part of my job to get there in time. There's not a *ritard.* at the end, so we do want to keep it in time and we do actually want to get to this silently depressed chord, and carefully catch it in time, and then release the pedal in time. There's a fermata on that last chord so you can hold it a little longer. But I would still count and know how much longer I'm holding that fermata for.

> *This piece functions within a limited gamut of notes, but Cage finds incredibly inventive ways to keep us interested and to keep the piece full of variety*

Recognized as a leading interpreter of American music, Adam Tendler has performed extensively throughout the US, including at the Lincoln Center and Carnegie Hall. A graduate of Indiana University, he serves on the piano faculty of New York's Third Street Music School Settlement – the country's first community music school

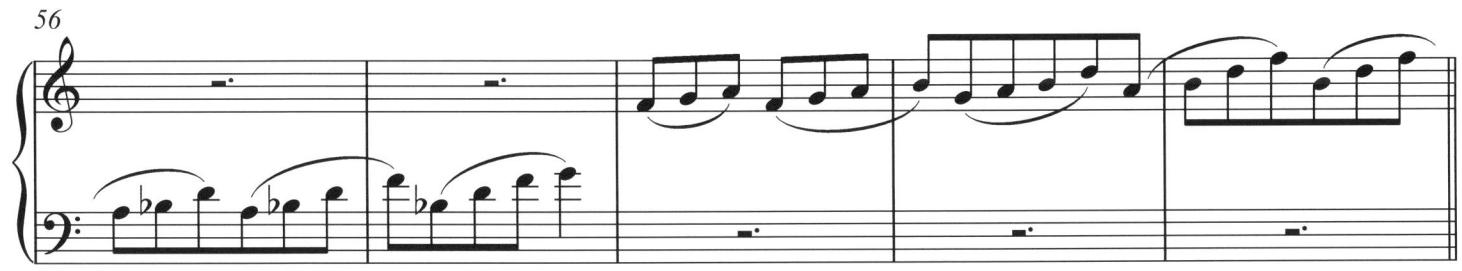

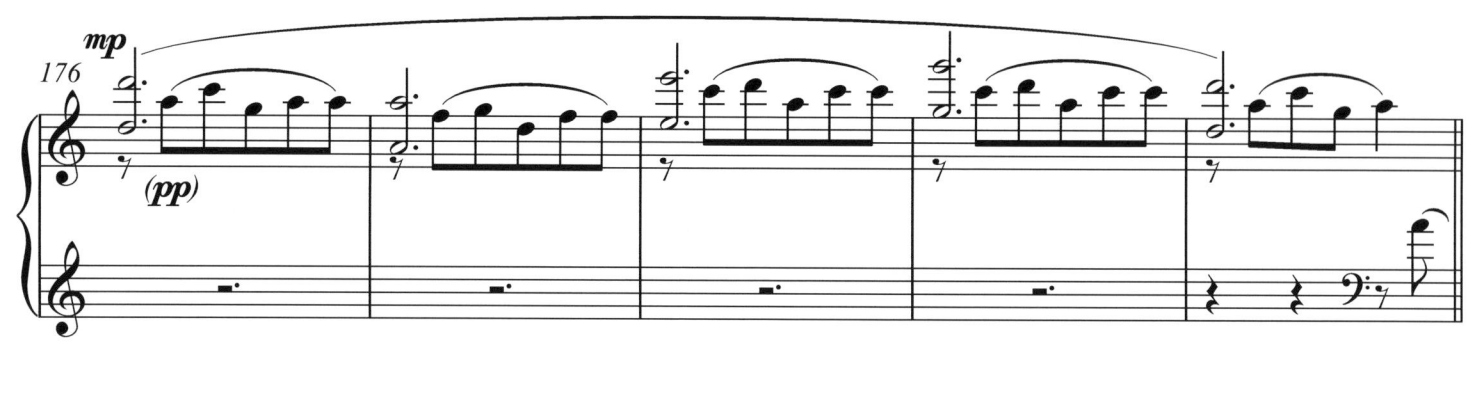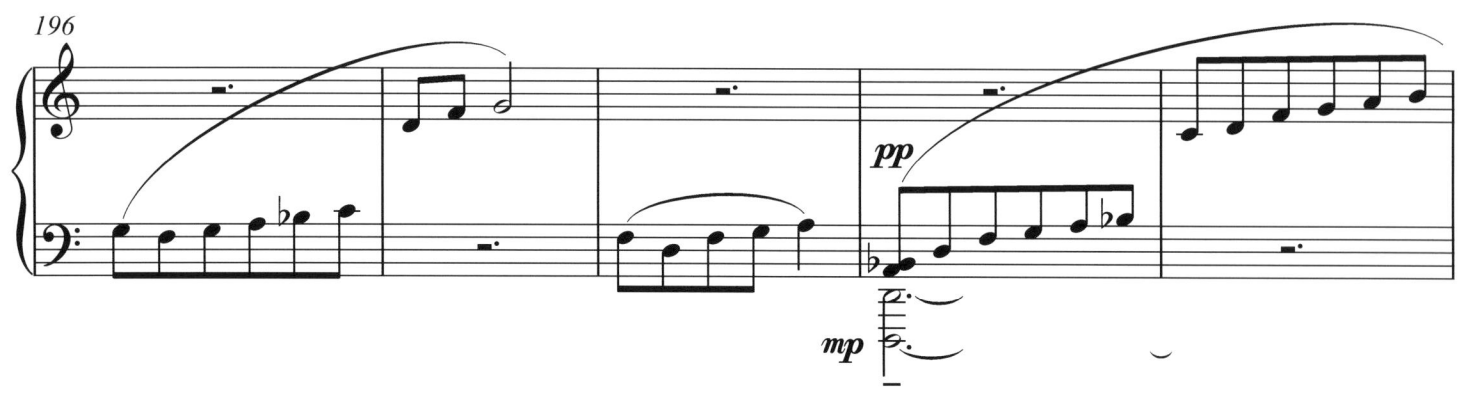

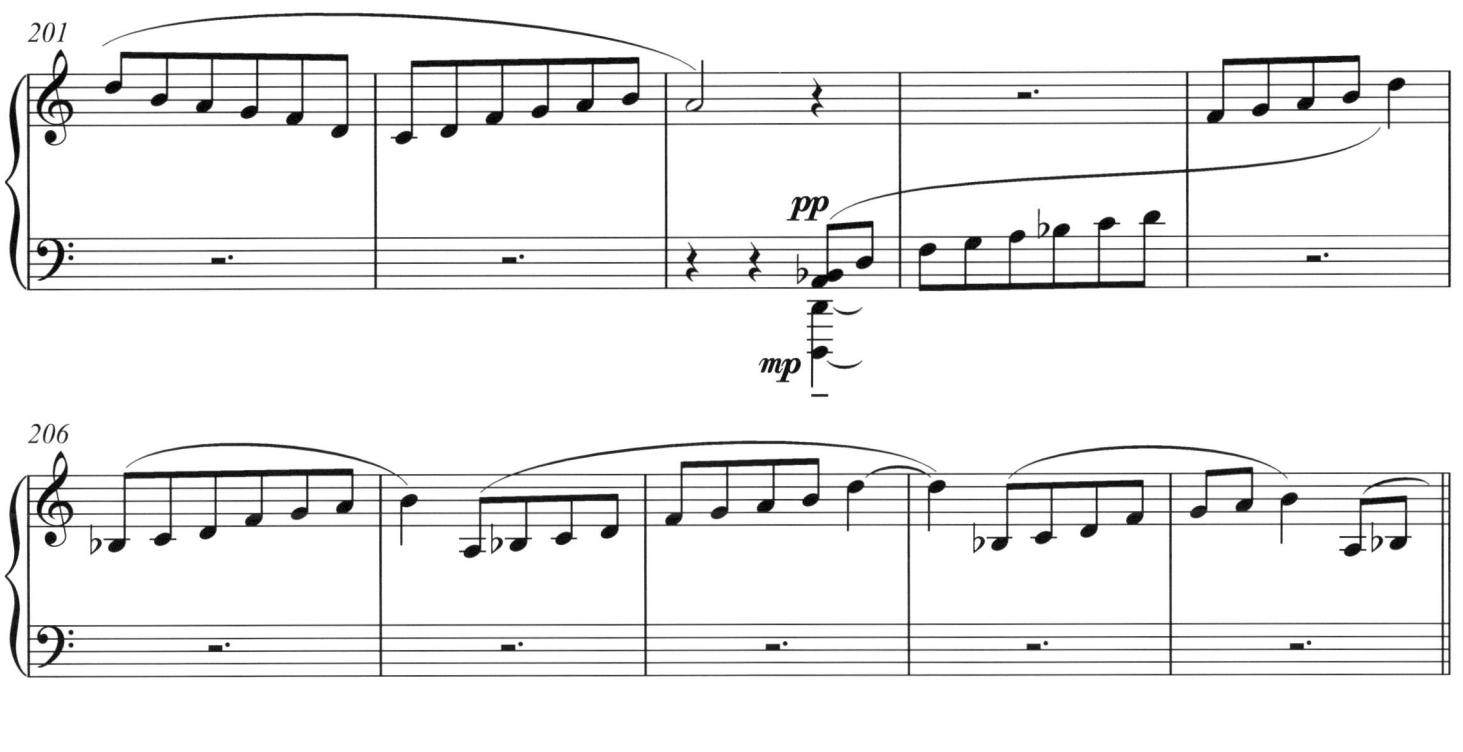

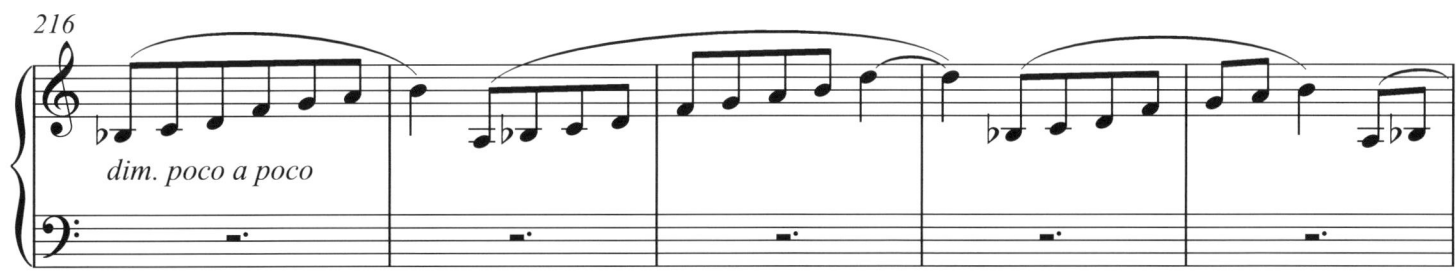
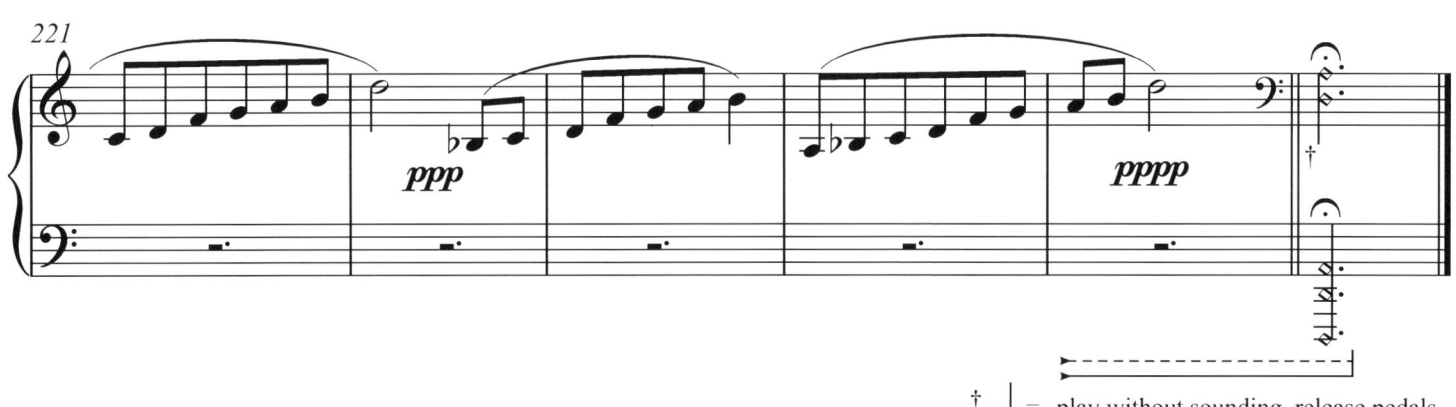

† 𝅗𝅥 = play without sounding, release pedals (thus obtaining harmonics).

About John Cage…

John Cage was born in September 1912 in Los Angeles. His ideas about music have been widely influential, including redefining the notion of 'composer' itself. His music emphasized rhythm and timbre over harmony, leading him first to focus on percussion.

The late 1940s saw musical refocusing – Cage's music became generally quieter, more delicate and he became very interested in Indian philosophy. He moved away from Western ideas of music as self-expression.

Cage continued to innovate and to explore. The early 1950s saw a series of pieces whose titles simply gave their durations and whose content was derived by means of various chance operations.

Cage later burrowed back into America's past, both musically and philosophically. It was presented by means of a score which was not concerned with specifying which notes should be played or sung, but rather with enabling performers to create a musical situation that was in itself interesting and expressive. Cage died in New York City in August 1992.

John Fallas

John Cage, New York 1983. Photograph by James Daubney, courtesy of the John Cage Trust

Merce Cunningham (far right) with Douglas Dunn (left) and Carolyn Brown (rear) on the Shiraz Art Festival, Persepolis Event 1972

In a Landscape…

The premiere of *In a Landscape* was at Black Mountain College, North Carolina, on 20 August 1948, when Cage played it to accompany dances choreographed by Louise Lippold. The structure Lippold gave him for *In a Landscape* is reflected in 15 groups of 15 bars each, and each of those 15-bar units is itself subdivided into 5+7+3 bars.

The music consists of a small number of different types of pattern. These are swapped between the hands to make different combinations of melody and accompaniment comprised of what Cage called a 'gamut', a fixed pool of pitch options set up in advance by the composer. In the closing bars a *diminuendo* leads to the final chord, which Cage asks you to play so gently that the notes do not sound at all. You will hear, not the five notes of the chord, but overtones or harmonics. Thus the piece ends by revealing a kind of secret hidden within the sound.

John Fallas